Speak Now

OR FOREVER

Rest In Peace

THE VERY REAL DANGERS OF HMOS — & WHAT YOU CAN DO ABOUT THEM

GORDON MILLER, M.D. WITH **TOM MANN**

ILLUSTRATIONS BY **MICHAEL RUSSELL** WITH **S. W. CONSER**

BOOK DESIGN BY MICHAEL RUSSELL

CONTENTS

Disclaimer

T his book is a critique of the managed-care industry. The opinions expressed are those of the author, and do not necessarily represent the views or opinions of any other person associated with, or included in, this work.

A number of terms used in this book are intended to have broad meanings. A glossary has been included so that there is no confusion as to the specific meaning of terms used within these pages.

On occasion, both hypothetical and anecdotal stories are used to illustrate points in this work. Anecdotal stories are footnoted as such, while hypothetical scenarios are left to the reader's imagination.

Unless otherwise footnoted at the end of the paragraph, characters and situations created in this work are fictional. Any resemblance to a living person or actual event is purely coincidental and unintended.

FOREWORD

BY GORDON A. MILLER, M.D.

....

I come from a family of health-care professionals. My father was an old country doctor, my mother is a nurse, and my brother and sister, and many uncles and aunts are also in the health-care field. Growing up, I watched my father and learned about the doctor-patient relationship. Today, as an ophthalmologist, I certainly don't claim to practice the best ophthalmology in the world—but I do claim to practice the best ophthalmology that I know. And like my father, I also practice in the traditional medical ethic (Hippocratic Oath), which requires me to have a *covenant* relationship with my patients. This relationship is the hallmark of being a true professional. By a covenant relationship I mean I am required to do the maximum I am able to do for my patients.

Unfortunately, the covenant relationship that defines a true professional is becoming extinct. As health care shifts its emphasis from the needs of the patient to an obsession with cost control and profit, the traditional medical ethic has been replaced. Instead of doctors having covenant relationships with their patients, they now have contractual relationships—that is, doctors now do for their patients the minimum they can get away with in order to fulfill the contract.

Nowhere is this contract mind-set more prevalent than in the managed-care system of medicine, better known as Health Maintenance Organizations, or HMOs. With their fascination with cost controls and profit, HMOs have, by in large, implemented a system of perverse financial incentives designed to limit care to patients. Because this is a direct attack on the traditional medical ethic practiced throughout the ages, I have dedicated myself to stopping HMOs from implementing capitation and other perverse financial incentives. It is my firm belief that these immoral financial incentives are used to deny patients access to timely necessary care.

My father taught me that, in traditional medical ethics, your doctor is your advocate. However, under capitation and other perverse financial incentives, your doctor is the advocate for the HMO, not for you, the patient. This 180-degree turn has resulted in disaster for patients. In fact, a recent national study in the Journal of the American Medical Association noted, "The health outcomes were significantly worse for chronically ill, elderly and poor patients treated in HMOs..." than those treated in traditional medical institutions.[3]

But you'll never hear that from your HMO or the contracted doctors they've bought off. You see, HMOs have doctors sign contracts containing "gag" clauses that don't allow doctors to tell you everything you should know about your health. The truth is, HMOs are hoping you never find out that the more care your doctor denies,

the more money he makes under their perverse financial arrangements.

Under traditional medical ethics, doctors do whatever they are able to do for the individual patient, regardless of the patient's status in life. Now with HMO-created perverse financial incentives, doctors practice under a *"veterinary ethic"*—that is, they do for you only what your master or owner allows. In other words, they treat you like a dog! Your master or owner in the case of managed care is the party paying your medical bills: your HMO, your insurance company, or the government. Under this system, which created gag clauses and perverse financial incentives, you're not supposed to find out that what really matters is profit, not lives!

Did you know that HMO executives make 62 percent more in salary and bonuses than their corporate peers? This is money that should have been spent on your health-care needs. But HMO executives line their pockets with blood money, while at the same time claim to lower health care costs. However, HMOs are not really saving us any significant money. According to the American Medical Association, the whole of managed care is only saving us between **ZERO and 3.9 percent!** The AMA further states that it found, *"...no evidence that managed care, in any form, has reduced the rate of growth in national health-care expenditures."* [43] [40]

Obviously, I want to ban the perverse financial incentives implemented by HMOs. But, this isn't about money, it's about the ethics of health care, and ensuring that patients can trust their doctors to give them the health care they need when they need it. Perverse financial incentives, such as capitation, are vandals within the gates of medicine—pillaging the heart and soul of a profession while leaving behind a trail of shattered lives and cold bodies of those who needed medical care, but were denied. Paying a doctor more money when he deliberately denies you care is clearly wrong. And my dad taught me that there is never a right way to do the wrong thing.

This book is intended to help you become a better-informed patient. But I also hope to light a fire within you—so that you, too, become a passionate voice crying against the betrayal of the chronically ill, the elderly and the poor by the medical industrial complex.

It is clear to me that the government is not going to protect the people from the managed care industry which has sold out its ethics. The government has apparently sided with the managed care industry in no small part due to fat political contributions. I believe the only way things will improve is if "We the People" do something about it. So speak now—or you may forever rest in peace.

DOMINE MISERERE NOBIS

"Speaking as one colleague to another, it appears that you've sold your soul. Unfortunately, that's not covered by our HMO."

CHAPTER 1

WHAT'S HAPPENING AT YOUR HMO?

"Shocked and outraged" would be the only way to describe viewer reaction to a Los Angeles-based investigative television show with Ed Bradley. The veteran *60 Minutes* host used his new program, *Street Stories*, to investigate disturbing allegations involving *Health Maintenance Organizations,* or *HMOs.* What Bradley and his crew discovered was a system that routinely placed patients in danger of losing their lives. [1]

Viewers cringed as they learned of a doctor who decided for himself when his senior-citizen patients had "lived long enough." As alleged by a former colleague, this doctor changed the orders for a heart-attack patient, no longer allowing that patient to be resuscitated—that is, to be brought back to life. He explained his actions by telling his colleague, "You're costing me too much d**n money!"

The colleague went on to explain that saving people's lives is expensive—and that HMOs are more worried about making money than saving lives.

What Bradley may not have realized was that he'd only found the tip of the iceberg. His show wasn't the first, and it certainly won't be the last, in exposing the horrific consequences of HMO policies—policies that reward doctors who save money instead of lives. In fact, stories such as Bradley's have been reported throughout the media, from the *Los Angeles Times* to *Donahue,* from *60 Minutes* to *The New York Times.* Yet HMOs continue to grow around the country, currently boasting a user membership of more than 50 million, with an expected growth of an additional 50 million people by the year 2000. [2]

Health Maintenance Organizations, or HMOs, are more concerned about making money than saving lives.

So when physicians and members of the media are drawing attention to managed care's aggressive financial policies—policies that can put patients at risk—why are so many Americans willing to join? The answer can be broken into two parts:

• First, *Americans are not choosing HMOs—their employers are.* And these employers are more concerned about the cost of their insurance package than they are about quality of care.

• Second, *managed care is only potentially dangerous to people who are sick and try to use the service.* However, the overwhelming majority of people in America are healthy, meaning they have little

HMOs create a perverse system we'll call "Medical Darwinism"—where only the healthy are allowed to survive.

interaction with HMOs save the occasional office visit. Thus, they fail to see the managed-care threat.

These two facts have caused the insurance pendulum to swing violently toward HMOs—so violently, in fact, that the medical profession is no longer primarily concerned with curing the ill. Instead, *bean counters are running our medical system*— with the goal of making money for themselves and their stockholders.

But what about those who are really sick? As reported by the American Medical Association, the elderly and poor fare significantly worse under managed-care arrangements. And there are plenty of horror stories (or "negative outcomes," as HMOs call them) throughout the country to suggest that the sick can be in serious danger when subjected to aggressive managed care. The reason is simple: *It's expensive to care for the ill, and the HMO industry is about saving money—which means that the philosophy of quality care is in direct conflict with the philosophy of HMOs.* The unfortunate reality for the sick is that the buyers of health care (employers, the government, and insurance companies) have fallen in love with HMOs because of their affordability, and have conspired with HMO organizations to put more and more people into them. [3]

This doesn't mean that we have to simply sit back and take it. As in the past, when the consumer has been abused, there are ways to put the brakes on a perverse system. In this case, a perverse system that rewards those who save costs instead of lives.

This book is intended to give the reader a glimpse of the inner workings of health care under its new rules. It will show that these new, HMO-created rules lead to a perverse system we'll call *"Medical Darwinism"*—a twisted setup in which only the healthy are allowed to survive. We'll also compare Medical Darwinism to the original framework and philosophy of medicine, where every patient was individually treated to the best of his or her physician's ability.

It's important to note that a perfect system of medicine has yet to be created. However, the goal of any "reform" is to enhance the performance and outcome of a given system. In the case of medicine, the HMO "reforms" have turned out to be worse than the original illness.

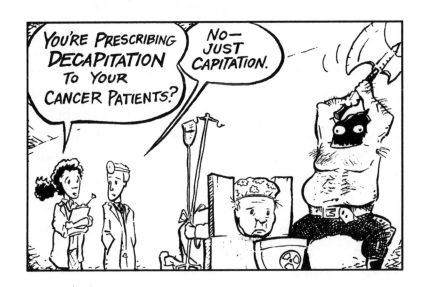

Chapter 2

What is an HMO?

An HMO is specifically designed to limit your access to health care through a variety of methods—including paying your primary-care, or "gatekeeper," doctor to deny you access to tests, specialists, hospital stays, and other procedures. Aggressive managed care gives rise to four distinct issues that potentially put patients at risk for their very lives.

If you hope to survive your encounter with a Health Maintenance Organization, or HMO, we suggest you remember the Boy Scout motto—"Be Prepared." To help familiarize you with some of the potential dangers you may face at your HMO, it's important to first understand what an HMO is and how it works.

An HMO usually works something like this: You or your employer pay a premium to your health carrier, which in turn contracts your health-care needs out to an HMO. Within the HMO, you are assigned a primary-care doctor, or "gatekeeper." Your gatekeeper may be in charge of as many as 1,000 patients like yourself. As a policyholder, you can only see your primary-care gatekeeper doctor. The HMO gives him or her the authority to control all your referrals, limiting your access to expensive tests, hospital stays, and specialists. That's why they're called "gatekeepers"!

The reason behind blocking your access to tests, hospital stays, and specialists is simply to save money. HMOs believe that when patients are able to see the specialist they want or get the test they want, there are no cost controls. By blocking the patient's access to these services, patients are no longer able to "drive" the health-care system. The gatekeeper decides for the patient when a specialist or test is needed.

But here's where a conflict arises: *By cutting down on specialists, tests, and hospital stays, the HMO*

If your primary-care physician is overly concerned with saving money, he or she can block your access to vital tests, referrals, and hospital visits.

saves money. In most cases, these gatekeeper doctors are given large financial incentives to limit your access. According to *Time* magazine, one group of gatekeeper doctors on the East Coast was offered $25,000 apiece if their group of patients used less than 180 days in the hospital—*regardless of each individual patient's health-care needs.* This may be the reason behind new mothers being kicked out of the hospital after one day, or outpatient "drive-through" mastectomy surgery, where the patient leaves the hospital just hours after this traumatic procedure. [4]

In some HMO systems, the gatekeeper gets a different financial incentive called *capitation*. This is a system where the gatekeeper gets a flat fee per person per month to take care of a group of patients. *Whatever money the gatekeeper doesn't spend on his patient's health care, he or she keeps. Whatever money he does spend, he or she loses.* Thus, the gatekeeper's incentive is to do as little as possible for his or her patients in order to maximize personal gain. (5)

As you can see, in the HMO system the primary-care gatekeeper runs the show (at least as far as you're concerned; the HMO exercises its own control over the physician, as we'll see later). In order to see a specialist or get a specific test, you need a referral from your gatekeeper. Sometimes it's easy to get the referral, sometimes it's not—it all depends on the individual gatekeeper and the HMO for which he or she works.

There are other tools HMOs use to limit your care. They have systems called *"Peer Review," "Utilization Boards,"* and *"Reviewers"* that all combine to make sure you don't get too much care—as defined by the HMO policy book.

Under the *Peer Review* system, doctors watch each other to make sure, among other things, that no doctor in the group is doing too many tests or sending too many patients to specialists. The reason these other doctors care so much about the actions of their colleagues is they all can share in a pool of money called a *withhold*. This withhold is a percentage of

Even if a gatekeeper *is* ethical, he or she may be subject to *Peer Review*, *Utilization Boards*, or *Reviewers*—bureaucratic mechanisms designed to make sure you don't get "too much" care.

money put into a pool by all the doctors to be used for patient tests, specialists, and other health-care needs. This pool of money is then combined with other pools of money from other groups within the HMO (such as the pharmacy group, the emergency room group, etc.). If the doctors don't use this money, they get to split it among themselves at the end of the year—and not just the money they put in; they all get a piece of the entire pot! This means they can actually get back much more money than they originally contributed … if they haven't blown it on patient care! But if one doctor in the group is doing too many tests or sending

HMOs have "formulas" for most ailments that dictate how much care they think you should receive.

too many patients to specialists, it decreases the amount of money the doctors will split at the end of the year. So, physicians are encouraged to watch each other to make sure no one doctor is spoiling the mix by giving too much care to his or her patients.

Gatekeepers also are watched by *Utilization Boards*. These boards, made up of both doctors and HMO bean counters, watch how much health care a doctor is giving. You see, HMOs have a care guideline—a formula, if you will—for just about every ailment. If you go in with a given ailment, the formula dictates how much health care you should get. If your doctor gives you more care than the formula "recommends," the Utilization Board may reprimand him or her for not abiding by HMO policy. If your doctor routinely ignores the HMO policy and gives you more health care than deemed necessary according to the HMO rules, your doctor may be fired outright for "over-utilizing."

The job of the *reviewer* is to decide whether or not the procedure your physician performed was actually necessary; if it wasn't necessary, the reviewer then decides whether or not to pay the bill. Doctors know they may not be paid under certain arrangements with the HMO if they record too many incidents of a certain procedure. So the reviewer acts as a sort of deterrent to giving the patient more care than deemed necessary—deemed necessary not by your doctor, but by the HMO rule book.

In short, the HMO is specifically set up to deny patients access to tests, specialists, hospital stays, and other procedures deemed unnecessary by the primary gatekeeper doctor and the HMO's policies and rules. HMOs use a variety of methods—including financial incentives, peer review, utilization boards, and reviewers—to ensure you don't get care they don't think you need. The bottom line is that neither the patient nor the doctor really decide what care is needed: the HMO decides for you.

Now that you've had a glimpse at how an HMO operates, let's take a look at the fundamental problems of this arrangement. There are four problem areas—which, if they succeed at their goal, will so radically change the basic doctor-patient relationship that every HMO participant, healthy or otherwise, should be alarmed.

1. MEDICAL PROVIDERS GET PAID FOR NOT WORKING.

As we've identified, HMOs were set up to control costs. Before the advent of aggressive managed care, the majority of doctors were paid through a system called "fee for service." In that system, a doctor was paid when he provided a service to his patient. This system of payment is much like you'd find anywhere in the marketplace: An auto mechanic gets paid for repairing your car; a dry cleaner gets paid for cleaning your clothes; and a doctor was paid for curing your illness.

The fact is that fee-for-service, or some variation on fee-for-service, is the traditional way physicians have been paid for their services since the advent of Western civilization. *In a fee-for-service system, the patient drives the system—because the patient is given access to tests, specialists, and procedures when the patient, along with the physician, feels they're necessary.* In a fee-for-service system, the patient plays an active role in defining his or her own health care, because the patient helps determine what care will be given—and

Under capitation, the way a physician makes the most money is by not treating any patients at all.

the physician receives payment for providing that care. [6]

Interestingly, though perhaps not surprisingly, HMOs frown upon this arrangement. The reason is rather simple: *HMOs are designed to limit a patient's access, while fee-for-service medicine is designed to enhance patient access.* In other words, the fee-for-service approach, which allows patients and their needs to drive the health-care system, is the exact opposite of what HMO executives want.

The concept of the HMO is really just a values shift within medicine. Instead of the patient's individual health-care needs taking center stage,

Under capitation, the physician—not the insurance company—is ultimately responsible for paying your medical bills.

so-called "costs savings and efficiencies" take the highest priority.

HMO managers took a hard look at the fee-for-service system and decided to turn it on its head. Instead of physicians being paid for performing services, as they had for thousands of years, just the opposite would happen: Doctors would *lose* money each time they provided a service! How the HMO manages this skewed system is quite clever, and it's called capitation.

As we discussed earlier, capitation is a payment method by which a physician is paid a set fee per patient per month. That pooled fee is then used to take care of that "population" of capitated patients. Thus, every time you need a service from your HMO primary-care gatekeeper, he or she has to pay for that service out of his or her pool of money. In other words, capitated physicians lose money when they treat you! On the other hand, if you don't see your gatekeeper, he or she keeps your monthly fee. The harsh reality of this system is that doctors make money from the healthy people who don't need their services, while they lose money on the sick who depend on them for a cure. This is Medical Darwinism at its worst: *Only the healthy survive in the HMO system; the sick are left to fend for themselves, because there's actually a financial incentive for the doctor to not take care of them!* In the end, your capitated provider gets paid for not giving you care. In fact, the way a capitated doctor makes the most money is not to see any patients at all. And you wonder why you can't get an appointment until next month!

2. THE FINANCIAL RISK OF EACH PATIENT IS SHIFTED FROM THE INSURANCE COMPANY TO THE DOCTOR.

In the old days, we used to buy health-care insurance to pay our medical bills should we get sick. But under aggressive managed care, that's no longer the case. As described above, one of the other consequences of paying a doctor via capitation is that the provider becomes responsible for paying your medical bills.

Let's say you get sick. You go to your gatekeeper, and he only has so much money in the bank from his pool of patients to spend on your care. But you're really sick, and in order to provide you the care you need, he'll have to spend everything he has in the bank, plus whatever other money he can find. But if he spends all that money on you, there will be no money left for his other patients. What does the doctor do? He either goes bankrupt or under-treats your condition in order to salvage whatever money he can.

Sound farfetched? Here's what happened to one HMO patient, as related by an orthopedic surgeon caught in the middle of an emergency:

" 'Mrs. Stevens' was referred by the Emergency Department physician to my orthopedic clinic after it was determined she had a broken arm which needed specialty care. However, she called to cancel her appointment, telling my receptionist that she was afraid her medical plan wouldn't pay for her visit. The receptionist checked with her supervisor and told Mrs. Stevens to keep her appointment and that we'd take care of her broken arm and worry about dealing with her southern-Californian HMO later.

"Several days before, Mrs. Stevens had fallen on

an outstretched arm while on vacation in Hawaii. She went to the local Emergency Room, X-rays were taken, a fracture was noted, she was given pain medication, a splint and sling were applied to her arm, and she was referred to a local orthopedic surgeon. Over the next day or two, the arm swelled—the splint was too tight—and she tried to make arrangements for follow-up. *Her southern-Californian HMO was contacted, but only 'emergency' treatment was authorized, and she was not allowed to go back to see the doctor.*

"Mrs. Stevens was told she would have to see a plan-approved doctor when she returned to southern California. To make matters worse, a family emergency arose which forced her to be away from her primary-care physician even longer. After a long flight to San Francisco, connecting flights, and an hour's drive up the Sacramento River canyon with a friend, Mrs. Stevens arrived in the little town of Dunsmuir. Every time she bumped her arm, it hurt—traveling made it worse—and finally she decided to go to the Emergency Room at the hospital in Mt. Shasta, where she was referred to me.

"The arm was bruised, but the swelling had decreased. Somewhere, the splint had been removed, and a sling provided only minimal fracture protection. While X-rays were being taken, my staff contacted the patient's HMO for emergency treatment authorization. Casting the arm would end the patient's pain, and also provide definitive treatment.

"*Treatment authorization was refused.* The HMO advised my staff to send the patient 600 miles south for treatment by a plan physician. I demanded to talk to the plan's medical-review physician. He reiterated his HMO plan's policy that Mrs. Stevens should have her arm treated by a plan physician in southern California.

"I explained that she had an unstabilized fracture, and that to send her 600 miles without proper treatment was cruel, inhumane, and below the standard of care. He told me there was nothing more he could do. Losing my patience, I told the doctor I already had cast the arm, and he could do you-know-what with his money. Then it hit me. 'Are you in financial trouble?' I asked. As it turns out, this capitated doctor was offered a 'sweet deal' by an HMO, but now, whatever the reason, they were out of money. He didn't even know how he was going to provide for his family, much less pay for treating Mrs. Stevens' arm. He thanked me for taking care of his patient, and for taking time to talk to him. He said he would send me payment if any money could be found. I never checked to see if he did." [7]

Under capitation, this is the risk both doctors and patients take. If the money runs out, both suffer the consequences. However, neither the HMO nor the insurance company suffer in this scenario. In fact, they make out like bandits—*because they no longer take the "risk" of your getting sick.* They don't have to pay for the broken arm—the primary-care doctor does, out of his capitated pool. The insurer and the HMO have already made their money off your premium and shifted the responsibility of paying for your care to the doctor under capitation. *The patient is the ultimate loser in capitated contracts, because there's no longer a guarantee the patient will get the care that's needed when it's needed!*

3. THE ETHICAL PROVIDER MUST MEET THE CONTRACT PRICE OF THE UNETHICAL PROVIDER WHO'S WILLING TO WITHHOLD MEDICAL CARE.

If it's not bad enough that capitation forces care to be withheld at some level, imagine what happens in the world of Medical Darwinism when two capitated doctors have to compete for the same patients. If there are two capitated doctors, and one is willing to take each patient for $10 per month, even though it means skimping on care, while the other needs to charge $30 per patient per month to actually cover the costs of patient care, which doctor will the HMO contract with? Obviously the low bidder!

An unethical doctor will accept an unreasonably low amount of money per patient from an HMO, driving down the quality of medical care. Are you getting your health care from the lowest bidder?

Just as obviously, though, an ethical doctor will never be able to meet the contract price of a physician willing to withhold care. Just as an HMO doctor can run out of money to treat a broken arm, an ethical doctor will go bankrupt if he or she provides all the care that's needed, because there simply isn't enough money in the HMO system earmarked for patient care.

A recent example of this underbidding process happened when an ophthalmologist was competing for an HMO contract. While the average price of eye care for each patient is about $15-$20 a month, this doctor told the HMO he could provide care to each of their patients for *50 cents a month*. For $6 per patient per year, this doctor said he would care for all these patients! There's no way this doctor can provide the care for what he's charging; he'll have to withhold standard medical care that ethical physicians wouldn't withhold. He may get the HMO contract, but he certainly won't be adequately treating any patients. [8]

As a patient, you have to remember that there's no such thing as a free lunch. A provider who underbids his competition is in effect admitting he will not provide as much care as his competitors. Are you getting your health care from the lowest bidder?

4. THE **HMO** SYSTEM ALLOWS FOR THE NON-MEDICAL CORPORATE PRACTICE OF MEDICINE.

Not that long ago, medical decisions were made between the doctor and the patient. As we've discussed, HMOs have constructed a system by which doctors are no longer allowed to use their medical judgment. Every decision a provider makes is reviewed, critiqued, and either approved or rejected by people who may not even be physicians! HMO rules often prohibit providers from even discussing treatment options with their patients. These rules were not put in place by the doctor, but by corporate bean-counters hoping to save money for their HMO.

Some HMOs are publicly traded on Wall Street—which means they're loyal to shareholders, not patients.

But these rules are just the tip of the iceberg when it comes to the non-medical corporate practice of medicine. Many HMOs are publicly traded on Wall Street; this means that the head of an HMO is ultimately responsible to a board of directors and stockholders demanding increased profits. The pressure to provide increased dividends to board members and stockholders drastically affects your health care.

Another thing that affects your health care is the *regionalization* of health-care services. HMOs aggressively recruit doctors to join their groups, and physicians are sucked up into this system as if it were a vortex—to the point where an entire region may be controlled by one HMO. When this happens in our region—witness the inroads made into Oregon's capitation industry by certain closed group practices—you may lose your choice of physician. Ask any of the thousands, perhaps millions, of HMO patients being forced to select a primary-care gate-keeper from a "provider directory" that fails to include the family doctor they've been seeing for years. [9]

When Wall Street and regionalization affect the type of health care a patient may receive—when corporations are playing doctor by limiting whom patients can see and (through their gatekeepers) what services they can get—you're faced with a system that allows for the non-medical corporate practice of medicine. And that's dangerous.

*In short, HMOs have created four major pitfalls that could put patients at risk: By allowing the provider to make more money by not providing care; by shifting the financial risk to the provider; by allowing unethical physicians to underbid health-care contracts; and by encouraging the non-medical, corporate practice of medicine; HMOs have put their patients in a very dangerous position. These patients are receiving health care from physicians who are financially encouraged **not** to deliver care to the "costly" sick—and their unethical, profitable allegiance to HMOs is forcing the entire health-care industry to follow them down a very deadly path.*

CHAPTER 3

FOLLOW THE MONEY

If you really want to get to the bottom of anything in today's world, you have to follow the money. Health care is no exception. Just how do HMOs steal money away from patient care and redistribute it to primary care doctors, corporate executives, and Wall Street investors? *Through a complex system of perverse financial incentives.*

Perverse financial incentives are a lot like sausage: The more you know about how they're made, the less you can swallow!

THE PERVERSE INCENTIVE
OF MANAGED CARE

Jill pays a monthly fee to her HMO/insurance company.

Jill finds a lump on her breast. She makes an appointment with her HMO primary-care "gatekeeper," Dr. Tom Jaeckel.

It turns out that Jill needs a mammogram— *but Dr. Jaeckel won't let her have one.*

What Jill doesn't know is that Dr. Jaeckel is a member of a *risk pool.* This pool of money is like a slush fund, to be used for tests (including mammograms), specialists, hospital stays, etc. The doctors get a year-end bonus, based on what they *don't* spend out of the risk pool. *In other words, if Dr. Jaeckel doesn't order too many mammograms, he makes a killing off the risk pool.*

As her primary-care gatekeeper, Dr. Jaeckel controls the vast majority of Jill's health-care dollars—based upon what services he chooses to offer or not offer. In a risk-pool arrangement, the less money a physician spends, the more money is returned to him or her at the end of the year...

...so instead of getting the mammogram she needs, Jill is sent home by Dr. Jaeckel. He tells her to "come back if there are any changes."

Because Dr. Jaeckel made this medical decision based upon money, not the needs of his patient, Jill may have a delayed diagnosis of cancer. As you can see, the risk-pool arrangement is a *perverse incentive*—because it uses money to influence care decisions.

THE DANGER OF
CAPITATION

Capitation can be even more dangerous than the perverse incentive. Here's an overview of how it works:

Edna pays a monthly fee to her "capitated" HMO.

After deducting a hefty profit for itself, the HMO gives the remaining money to Edna's primary-care physician, Dr. Tom Jaeckel. With this small per-patient sum, Dr. Jaeckel is expected to pay for *all* of Edna's health care.

Edna gets sick. After much wrangling, she finally gets an appointment with Dr. Tom...

...but thanks to capitation, Dr. Jaeckel gets paid less than it would cost to make Edna well. *He has to keep his treatment costs as low as possible—or he'll go broke treating the sick.*

Unfortunately, this can only lead to one thing...

...*Medical Darwinism—*where only the healthy are allowed to survive.

CHAPTER 4

THERE'S NEVER A RIGHT WAY TO DO THE WRONG THING

As practitioners of one of the first professions, healers have been charged with a special responsibility to care for their patients in a manner consistent with a code of ethics. The best-known of these codes is the Hippocratic Oath, the vow by which the majority of doctors abided before the advent of aggressive managed care. But the Hippocratic Oath has been tossed aside by the HMO community in favor of a new ethic—one that places the emphasis on making money instead of saving lives. (10)

A *bribe* is defined as something of value given to a person to persuade or induce them to do something—possibly something unethical. This definition applies to the medical profession when a health-care provider, who normally wouldn't withhold care from a patient, does so due to financial considerations.

A bribe is a bribe by any other name...including the names "capitation," "bonus," or "withhold." But to truly understand why there's never a right way to do the wrong thing, you have to take a quick look at the origins of the profession of medicine.

The word *profession* originates from the word *profess*, and has been widely associated with the clergy. In fact, it was men of the cloth who originally performed the duties of the four original *professionals*—teachers, healers, lawyers/mediators, and, of course, the clergy.

But there's more to a profession than simply professing knowledge—*there's a sacred relationship that forms between those who profess and those who receive the benefit of professional expertise.* Although in today's

An HMO physician violates *agency* by trying to work for both the patient *and* the HMO.

liberalized view of medicine this means very little, for centuries being part of one of the four professions meant conforming to the common-sense rules of ethics that went along with the title.

It's interesting to note that priests, lawyers, and doctors, as well as certain teachers, are among the handful of workers who take oaths pledging that they'll abide by ethical rules. Their professions are *that* important. As a member of a profession, you're automatically pledged to abide by the concepts of *Agency, Fiduciary Trust,* and *Informed Consent.* (11)

A quick look at the legal profession will help clarify these terms. Imagine you're an attorney. As an attorney, your job is to act on behalf of your client. This is called *agency*; you speak for your client and cannot work for anyone else—you can only act on behalf of one party at a time in any given conflict. Once you begin working for your client, you are then tasked with doing what's in the client's best interest. This is *fiduciary trust*—again, it means that not only do you speak for the client, but you do what's in the client's best interest and no one else's. Lastly, you must always tell your client of potential conflicts of interest; this is called *informed consent*. If, for example, you are personal friends with someone bringing suit against your client, you are morally bound by informed consent to tell your client about the friendship. Then it's up to the client to decide if he or she wants your services, given those circumstances.

So, then: *Agency (speaking for the client), fiduciary trust (doing what's in the client's best interest), and informed consent (being up-front with the client) are the cornerstones of professional representation.*

Now let's apply these terms to the medical profession. The "professional" is now a physician instead of a lawyer, and the "client" is now a patient. Under *agency*, the physician represents the patient and no one else (remember, he can only be the agent for one client at any one time). The physician's *fiduciary*

PROFESSIONAL PLEDGE No. 2: FIDUCIARY TRUST

I'M CONSIDERING SHORTENING YOUR HOSPITAL STAY TO, SAY...

THIS AFTERNOON.

...THIS AFTERNOON!

An HMO physician violates a patient's *fiduciary trust* by not always doing what's in the patient's best interest.

responsibility is to do what's in the best interest of the patient. And finally, the physician must give *informed consent* to the patient regarding information which is important to the patient's decision-making ability.

Pretty simple—that is, until you factor in the HMO variable.

*Under the HMO formula, the physician becomes the agent of the HMO or corporation for which he works, while at the same time **pretending** to be the agent of the patient.* But as we've learned above, a professional cannot be the agent for two clients at the same time—especially

PROFESSIONAL PLEDGE No. 3: INFORMED CONSENT

I'M BEGINNING TO THINK YOU'RE UNDULY INFLUENCED BY MY INSURANCE COMPANY, "DOCTOR."

WELL, SINCE YOU BROUGHT IT UP, I... HUH?

OH.

NEVER MIND.

GAG CLAUSE

An HMO physician violates *informed consent* by withholding vital information from the patient— on orders from the HMO.

when the clients have a natural conflict, i.e., one client needs medical care and the other client is paying the bill for that care. Obviously, the person needing the care wants the *best* that can be provided, while the payer wants the *least expensive* that can be provided. Having the doctor act as the agent of both the HMO/insurance company and the patient is like having a lawyer represent both the plaintiff and defendant at a trial—*it is impossible!*

The doctor's *fiduciary responsibility* is also split in the HMO arrangement. He or she must abide by company policy that may not be in the best interest of his or her patients—especially when it comes to the battle between quality care and the bottom line. When HMO policy overrules a physician's judgment as to what's in the best interest of the patient, fiduciary trust has been violated—which, unfortunately, happens daily!

And then there's *informed consent*. Many HMOs around the country have used what's called a *gag clause* in their contracts with physicians. In effect, these gag clauses prohibit a physician from saying or implying anything negative about their patient's HMO. Under an HMO gag clause, doctors might be prohibited from telling their patients about treatment options not covered by their HMO, financial incentives given by their HMO to limit care, specialty referrals, and expensive tests. *They can even, in some cases, prohibit doctors from telling their patients they need a second opinion!* This obviously violates informed consent.

How do HMOs get away with it? Simple. Even though ethics are unbreakable rules within a profession that define that profession, ethics are not law. Here's another example of the ethics of health care being perverted, as reported by KPTV in Portland, Oregon: [12]

Donovan Bass works at KPTV as a director of one of their news programs. Although an athletic and healthy man, Donovan began experiencing back pain and went to his HMO gatekeeper for help. The doctor examined Donovan; however, she didn't perform any tests such as X-rays or blood or urine samples. Donovan was told his back was okay—if anything, it may have been a slipped disk.

Donovan's pain not only continued, it increased—to the point where he couldn't get out of bed to go to work. He and his wife pleaded with the gatekeeper for a test called a Magnetic Resonance Imaging, or MRI, which is more sensitive than an X-ray. The doctor refused and, according to Mrs. Bass, told her the reason was that the test was too expensive—it cost about $1,000. At the time, Donovan and his wife did not know their gatekeeper was capitated.

The pain, however, didn't go away, and Donovan demanded an MRI. The doctor relented and scheduled the procedure. Several months had gone by before this test was finally scheduled. When the test was over, the technician looked pale, according to Donovan's televised interview. The tech told Donovan to call his gatekeeper. He did, and the gatekeeper apologized and told Donovan he had terminal cancer and would die. This cancer could have been found earlier had the gatekeeper been willing to provide either the MRI or blood and urine tests after Donovan's first visit.

The gatekeeper refused to be interviewed by KPTV. However, the station quoted her as saying, *"Money plays a role in every medical decision."*

Ethically, what went wrong here?

AGENCY: A doctor is supposed to be the patient's sole advocate. Instead, the doctor stonewalled the patient and didn't provide needed tests because it cost the company too much money. Obviously, the doctor was trying to act as agent for both the patient and the insurance company—siding more with the company in this case than with her patient.

FIDUCIARY TRUST: The doctor was supposed to do what was in her patient's best interest, but instead actually told the patient the tests were too expensive and unnecessary. Again, the doctor was looking out for the best interest of the company (and maybe herself, under her capitated arrangement) instead of the patient. Clearly, the MRI or even less-expensive tests were in the patient's best interest, but weren't given, probably because "money plays a role"—an unethical role—in her decision. [13]

INFORMED CONSENT: The doctor didn't inform the patient that the HMO had internal rules regarding expensive tests, and betrayed her patient by not giving informed consent regarding her financial arrangements with the HMO, i.e., financial arrangements that equated money spent with money lost. By not disclosing this important information, she violated informed consent.

RESULT: She betrayed her professional ethics and violated the patient's trust, and he'll die.

The disturbing part about the above story is that it's turned out to be commonplace within today's medical culture. But not every doctor sees things the HMO's way. That's because for the past 2,500 years there's been an ethical standard by which most doctors abided. And some doctors—those brave enough to challenge the HMO community—still practice ethical medicine according to these long-standing norms.

"Do No Harm"

Since the beginning of civilization, the concept of medicine or healing has implied helping, not hurting, those in need. Although evidence of medicine and healing practices reach back to 8000–3000 B.C., it's the Greek physician Hippocrates (460–370 B.C.) who's credited with founding the principles of our modern medical practice. [14]

Perhaps you've heard of the Hippocratic Oath, the ethical directions given to physicians regarding treatment of their patients. There are three main points to the Oath:

(1) A physician will only do those things which

are medically necessary for their patient and will do no harm;

(2) A physician will only perform those medical services at which he or she is skilled, bringing in specialists when necessary;

(3) All information shared between the doctor and patient, medically related or otherwise, will be confidential.

For 2,500 years, the vast majority of physicians have stood by this sacred oath. *But with the advent of aggressive managed care, all three of these ethical points have been tossed aside.* No longer are physicians doing everything they can for their patients; indeed, in many cases they're causing harm, as the case studies clearly show. (See Chapter 6, "The Cost of Progress," for several real-life horror stories.)

Because many HMO doctors actually lose money when they refer a patient to a specialist, they're provided with an overwhelming incentive to not do so. And when they don't refer patients to the specialists they need, these doctors violate their Hippocratic Oath to perform only those services at which they're skilled. In many cases, primary-care doctors are not sufficiently educated to make complex medical decisions dealing with, say, heart conditions or cancer. And lastly, non-medical HMO executives, reviewers, and even secretaries now have access to

An HMO throws out the Hippocratic Oath and replaces it with a "veterinary oath": *I will do for the patient only those things for which its master or owner is willing to pay.*

your confidential medical files, and know as much about you as your doctor, simply by pulling your chart up on a computer. Some health-care providers are even sharing your private medical records with your employer! This blatant breach of confidentiality completes the perversion of the Hippocratic Oath!

It's not that the HMO community has completely forsaken ethics; they've simply turned the Hippocratic Oath on its head. The perceived new ethic is what could be called the "Veterinary Ethic," and it goes something like this: *I will do for the patient only those things for which its master or owner is willing to pay.*

In other words, you're treated like a dog! And in the case of managed care, the "master" or "owner" is your employer, your insurance company, the government, or your doctor—none of whom, under HMOs, have a personal stake in your health. (15)

No doubt, Hippocrates is rolling in his grave.

But why the 180-degree turnaround? Why does the patient come last on Medical Darwinism's brutal food chain? In an attempt to bamboozle you, the HMO community has told you that the only reason they've created this system is because fee-for-service medicine doesn't work—regardless of the fact that it's been around since the beginning of medicine. In fact, HMO executives have the gall to argue that their way of delivering medicine is even better than the old way. In their twisted logic, HMOs argue that paying a doctor to *provide* a service is actually worse than paying a doctor for *withholding* a service!

This book is not suggesting that fee-for-service or any other health-care system is perfect. It isn't. But HMOs are not the solution their creators would like you to believe they are, and in fact they create infinitely more dangerous problems for the sick. You only have to ask yourself one critical question:

"Do I want my doctor to be paid for providing a service for me, or do I want my doctor to be rewarded by an HMO for withholding services from me?"

To be cured or not to be cured—that is the question.

In short, the ethics that guarded the profession of healer have been tossed to the wind by the HMO executives and HMO doctors willing to sell their souls to the highest bidder. Ethics are in place to protect not only the integrity of the profession, but to protect the public from a profession run amuck. In the current climate of HMO-induced Medical Darwinism, no one is safe.

"Any physicians who don't refer their patients to specialists for a year will receive this handsome set of steak knives."

C H A P T E R   5

THE BUY-OFF

Excessive financial influence on health-care providers within the HMO system is causing patients to be injured and even killed by the very medical profession charged with saving their lives.

"I wish to begin by making a public confession: In the spring of 1987, as a physician, I caused the death of a· man." This was the testimony of Dr. Linda Peeno, a former HMO medical reviewer, as she addressed the United States Congress. Dr. Peeno continued, "Although this was known to many people, I have not been taken before any court of law or called to account for this in any professional or public forum. In fact, just the opposite occurred: I was 'rewarded' for this. It brought me an improved reputation in my job, and contributed to my advancement afterwards. Not only did I demonstrate I could indeed do what was expected of me, I exemplified the 'good' company doctor: I saved a half-million dollars!...The primary ethical norm is: Do no harm. I did worse: I caused a death. Instead of using a clumsy bloody weapon, I used the simplest, cleanest of tools: my words. The man died because I denied him a necessary operation to save his heart. I felt little pain or remorse at the time. The man's faceless distance soothed my conscience. Like a skilled soldier, I was trained for this moment. When any moral qualms arose, I was to remember: **I am not denying care, I am only denying payment.***"* [16]

Welcome to the world of managed care. As we've discussed in previous pages, one of the top concerns of the HMO community is to save money, which really means "to make more money for the corporation." As Dr. Peeno now freely admits, HMOs are more than willing to reward health-care providers who go along with the program. In

HMO executives want you to believe that *they* should be determining the "appropriate" amount of care for patients.

fact, buying off these providers to withhold health care from you is the key to their success.

Let's take a quick look at the economics of medicine. Everything costs something in medicine. The more procedures a doctor performs, the more it costs. So HMO executives tell you they'll save you a lot of money if you'll just let them decide what the "appropriate" amount of care will be for patients.

Unfortunately, in order to save money in medicine, you have to provide less care—and because HMO executives are determined to save money, they're also determined to skimp on care. So how do they get the doctors to go along with denying care and access to their patients? That's where perverse financial incentives such as capitation come in. By financially rewarding doctors to withhold care and access, the HMO community has solved its last problem by buying off the only obstacle standing in the way of limiting your access to care—your doctor.

Now, let's take a look at capitation and how it works. As you know, instead of your doctor getting paid every time he does something for you, capitation means he gets a flat fee per month for you, and whatever he spends out of that fee, he loses. On the other hand, whatever he doesn't spend, he keeps. HMO executives spin the argument and say they now pay their doctors to keep you healthy. On the surface, it doesn't sound that devious. But let's look at this arrangement another way.

Suppose a man makes a contract with his neighbor that he'll buy her groceries every month. The neighbor will give him $100, and he'll go to the store and buy her food. But here's the catch: *Whatever's left over from that $100 is his to keep.* Now you can imagine that the neighbor would like him to buy the best food he can for that $100. But if he buys all the things she wants, he could end up spending the entire $100 or more, leaving him nothing for his trouble. *So he has to decide how to balance what's good for his neighbor against how much money he wants to keep for himself.*

**Do you trust the person buying
your medical "groceries"?**

So he buys her hamburger or liver instead of steak this month. And he decides she really doesn't need peanut butter this month. And that she can get more servings from powdered milk than she does from bottled milk. In the end, he spends $55 and keeps $45. The neighbor may gag on the food he bought, but he *was* careful to meet her minimum nutritional requirements!

In the case of capitated HMO medicine, you end up giving your "grocery" money to the primary-care doctor, who in turn has to make these same difficult decisions: *How much health care do I give the patient, and how much do I want to keep for my trouble?*

Medicine used to represent a covenant between a physician and a patient, where the doctor would do everything possible for the good of the patient. *Today's HMOs have broken that covenant and replaced it with a contract.* Now a physician only has to meet the minimum requirements of that contract, regardless of the best interests of the patient. And in most cases, those HMO contracts calculate their dollar amounts based on the quantity of patients covered, not the quality of care for those patients.

How many of you would actually allow your neighbor to do your grocery shopping under these conditions? If so, why do you let your doctor operate like this? Now can you see why gatekeepers might want to keep you from specialists, tests, hospital stays, and procedures?

Capitation is not the only perverse incentive health-care providers receive in payment for denying you care. As we've previously discussed, there are also *bonuses* and *withholds*, where doctors receive money as a "reward" for not using tests, specialists, hospital stays, and procedures. The entire system is set up to pay your doctor for limiting your care. Remember the most basic medical economics: The more you do, the more it costs; the less you do, the less it costs. Under the terms of aggressive managed care, that "cost" is borne by the doctor—who, instead of treating you based on your medical needs, is *not* treating you based on his or her bottom line.

With *bonuses* and *withholds*, physicians get money for *not* using tests, hospital stays, and procedures.

It may seem like we're picking on doctors. That's because *it's largely their fault: If the majority of doctors weren't so willing to sell their souls to HMO conglomerates, we wouldn't be where we are today.*

HMO apologists like to say that there was greed in the system long before they took over, and that HMOs were created to stop greedy fee-for-service doctors. But those "greedy" fee-for-service doctors were never given a bonus for denying you care. Those "greedy" fee-for-service doctors were never paid more money for not seeing you. And those "greedy" fee-for-service doctors weren't given huge bonuses for not referring you to specialists.

In summary, HMOs have put your life in danger by encouraging your health-care provider to skimp on your care—either by making the provider financially responsible for the "risk" of your getting ill (capitation) or by paying the provider large sums of money for not utilizing certain services (via bonuses and risk pools).

CHAPTER 6

HMOs Say: "Doctors and Patients are the Problem!"

Within the HMO culture, it's believed that patients, along with their doctors, are the real problem behind America's rising health-care costs. According to the HMO bean-counters, insured patients aren't paying all the bills for their health care, and they don't care about rising costs. So in order to keep costs down, *these same bean-counters believe that patients should be taken out of the health-care equation.* The HMO will decide their health-care needs instead.

Up to now, we've spent a lot of time talking about HMOs, doctors, and our current system of medicine as compared to medicine as it was originally, ethically conceived. But what role do you, the patient, play in all this? What responsibility, if any at all, does the patient have regarding his or her health? And why should a patient care about the radical changes that are transforming medicine in today's society?

These are important questions—not from an academic standpoint, but from the standpoint that each one of us, at some point, will be a patient. You may be healthy right now, but consider your fate down the road. Or consider the fate of a loved one—an elderly parent, or a spouse diagnosed with cancer—in light of what you've learned about how some HMOs operate. What can you do to ensure you get all the medical care you need *when you're the patient* if the system is set up to discourage your needs?

"...Patients can't drive [the system] any more; patients can't decide, 'My ear hurts, so I'm going to the doctor today.'" This according to William Popek, an HMO bigwig who makes no secret of wanting to decide your health-care needs for you. Take a moment

Even HMO executives admit it—they want to erase the patient from the health-care equation.

and think about his statement. If you feel sick, you're no longer allowed, under the HMO scenario and according to Popek, to decide for yourself to go to the doctor. And you thought this was America! [17]

Taking the patient out of the health-care equation created a fundamental change in how medicine is practiced in this country. From the HMO's perspective, the reason for taking the patient out of the game is simple: *The patient always wants health care, and the more care they seek, the more it costs.* By taking the patient out of the driver's seat, they've more or less eliminated the demand for health care—leaving that to be decided by a local HMO administrator with

In order to justify their unethical "cost-cutting" measures, HMOs needed someone to blame— so they chose you and your doctor.

a quarterly budget. That's why HMOs have set up their organizations the way they have, and why doctors have been forced to give up the traditional practice of ethical medicine.

As the history of medical ethics shows, from Hippocrates on down, the practice of medicine was never intended to shut out the individual patient. Now that you know something about these ethics, you can understand the rank injustice facing patients across the country who no longer have their choice of doctors, who have a difficulty convincing their doctor they need a certain test or procedure, and who can't get an appointment for months (if they even manage to get through a modern clinic's phone system!).

The reason you've been taken out of the health-care system is because HMOs needed a scapegoat, and you're it. The majority of Americans have some type of health-care coverage. The poor have government-sponsored health care (Medicare/Medicaid), while most middle- and upper-class families either have employer-based health insurance or have purchased individual policies. But in all these systems, the patient isn't the one paying most of the bill. There's a third party— insurance companies, employers, and the government—paying the bulk of the cost when you attend to your health-care needs.

Why is this? A primary reason is that during World War II, the federal government imposed a national wage freeze. In order to retain good workers, employers were allowed to offer health insurance benefits with *before-tax dollars* which were not counted against the freeze. Thus was born the third-party payer, who became responsible for paying our medical bills.

But as medicine became more expensive and more people began needing medical care (especially the growing elderly population), the cost to these third parties skyrocketed. Between 1980 and 1994, the cost of medical care increased 182 percent (this according to *The Oregonian*, Dec. 18, 1996). Studies began to show that 80 percent of health-care costs were due to six bad habits or lifestyle choices: alcohol, tobacco, illicit drugs, obesity, poor diet, and/or a promiscuous sex life. It was no longer financially viable to allow patients to decide what health care they wanted, because they were asking for all the latest procedures and breaking the bank. (18)

These are very real problems, and this book certainly isn't going to argue that such problems don't exist. But when it came time to look for solutions, the purveyors of HMOs waded into the debate and pointed their fingers at the parties that were simply too easy to blame—you and your doctor.

Without taking other factors into account—such as the increasing costs of research and development—insurance companies and their HMO accomplices convinced physicians, and the public, that rising costs meant people must be getting more health care than they actually needed, and that something had to be done. Well, they did something—they created aggressive managed care, where you no longer have a say in what health care you get.

But their quick and easy fix—which was never really intended to do anything but push more money the insurance company's way, as you'll see in later chapters—created an even larger problem. Instead of getting the health care they need, people are now being denied necessary care, which is causing injury and death.

**If HMOs chose your car
instead of your medical care....**

And they still haven't fixed the *real* problem in health care. That problem is the *third-party payers*—the insurance companies themselves.

Why are third-party payers part of the problem? Let's look at it this way: If someone told you that you could pick any car you wanted and they would buy it for you, would you keep the car you have, or would you buy a Mercedes, a BMW, or a Porsche? It's a similar scenario in medicine. If that car is medical care, then the HMO community has decided that you'll get a Yugo—with or without your approval. As far as HMOs are concerned, you no longer have the right to decide your own medical fate.

HMOs have also thrown an interesting rhetorical twist into their campaign against the patient: HMOs now say they focus on "preventive" medicine, and boast that their job is to keep you healthy. What they don't mention is that there's an obvious difference between keeping someone healthy who isn't sick in the first place, and making someone healthy who *is* sick. HMOs now freely admit that they no longer place a premium on healing the sick—they place a premium on those they can *keep* from getting sick.

A former president of the Oregon Medical Association actually crowed that medicine is no longer *about curing disease,* but just about keeping people healthy. He further argued that the patient has no role whatsoever in medical decision-making. Attitudes like his clearly affect how you're treated when you go see your primary-care gatekeeper. [19]

Here's an example of how this attitude might play out in an HMO setting: A woman goes to her gatekeeper after finding a lump on her breast. Her doctor tells her not to worry, it's nothing, and to keep an eye on it. The woman is a little put out by this— there's a history of breast cancer in her family—so she immediately asks for a mammogram. The doctor says it isn't necessary, even though mammograms are supposed to be "preventive medicine." A couple of months later, she returns and there's a second lump. Her doctor still refuses her mammogram request.

With their emphasis on "prevention," HMOs now freely admit that they no longer place a premium on healing the sick—instead, they place a premium on those they can *keep* from getting sick.

Not willing to take any more chances, the patient goes and gets a second opinion. The second doctor immediately does a biopsy and finds cancer. [20]

Why didn't the first doctor treat the patient? Two reasons: First, it costs money to do those tests. Second, it's no longer the HMO doctor's job to treat disease—he only works to keep people healthy.

If you think the above scenario sounds silly and paranoid, go on to the next chapter for some real-life examples.

In short, HMOs believe that patients are part of the health-care problem. Third-party payers of health care revolted against the increasing costs of medicine and demanded health-care reform that controlled these costs. Calls for reform are not unfounded, but where third-party payers went wrong was in turning to HMOs for a solution. The HMO community too-easily blames the patient, saying patients only want the best care somebody else is willing to pay for. But the resultant "solution" creates problems of an even more dangerous strain: Under the new HMO-style health care system, patients are no longer allowed to decide what health care they get. This new system encourages physicians to meet only the minimum health requirements within a one-size-fits-all formula—to do for the patient only those things for which its master or owner is willing to pay.

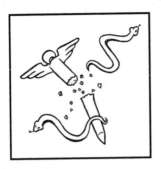

CHAPTER 7

THE COST OF "PROGRESS"

While HMOs across the country brag about their cost-saving ability, they rarely talk about who really pays the price for their cut-rate operations—the patients. There truly is no such thing as a free lunch, and many HMO patients have learned the hard way that the consequence of lower-cost medicine is lower-quality care. There are winners and losers in today's medicine. You've seen the winners—primary-care gatekeepers, HMO executives, insurance companies, Wall Street. Now meet some of the losers:

NELENE FOX

Hearing a diagnosis of breast cancer can be a woman's worst nightmare. That nightmare happened to Nelene "Nellie" Fox of Woodland Hills, Calif. Nellie was covered by her HMO, HealthNet, for such a tragedy. At least, that's what she thought.

HealthNet's contract with Nellie included coverage for bone-marrow transplants, a relatively new and expensive procedure to fight breast cancer. And HealthNet had $4.8 million in its transplant fund should a case such as Nellie's arise.

HealthNet denied her transplant request, and Nelene Fox died of breast cancer.

After Nellie's death, the family sued and won $89.1 million, the largest jury verdict ever against an HMO. A few hundred thousand dollars for the transplant could have saved her life, but all the money in the world can't bring back Nellie—the victim of an HMO that didn't want to spend the money to save her. [21]

JOYCE CHING

Joyce Ching's primary-care "gatekeeper" doctor was paid just $26.94 a month by Met-Life HMO to administer her health-care needs. Joyce was experiencing abdominal pains and rectal bleeding, but her "capitated" gatekeeper *decided not to do any extensive testing or examinations*, even though he found a mass in her abdomen—this according to the subsequent lawsuit filed by Joyce's husband, David.

According to David Ching, Joyce's gatekeeper and his partner *refused to allow her to see a specialist for her pain and bleeding*. They didn't refuse her request just once, but *six times* over the course of the following two-and-a-half months.

As a result, according to the family attorney, Joyce's undiagnosed but highly treatable cancer perforated her bowel and spread, leading to her death. (22)

ALICE THOMAS

Seventy-year-old classical pianist Alice Thomas of Portland, Ore., was told by her HMO doctor, and by the specialist he had sent her to see, that she needed surgery to repair nerve damage in her neck affecting her right arm and hand. *But the HMO's reviewers disagreed with her doctors, and denied payment for the procedure*, telling the doctor to prescribe less-expensive physical therapy instead.

The physical therapy was too little too late, and again her doctor requested that the HMO allow him to perform the surgery. This time, the HMO agreed.

Unfortunately for Alice, they didn't agree in time. The nerve damage had become so severe it couldn't be reversed. Alice Thomas can no longer play classical music or make adequate use of her claw-like right hand. The HMO settled with her, out of court, for $1 million. (23)

ELIZABETH QUIJARRO

The first time HMO-insured Elizabeth Quijarro went to her clinic complaining of chest pains, she did not see a doctor. A nurse practitioner examined her and later sent her home. The second time Elizabeth went to the same clinic with the same chest pains, she was directed to the same nurse practitioner, who had no specialized education in heart disease.

Like a drowning person repeatedly sinking underwater, Elizabeth never came back up on her third try. She suffered a massive heart attack the same morning she was scheduled to visit her clinic, where her HMO had promised her she would finally see an M.D. The heart attack cut off the flow of blood to her brain, leaving her a vegetable on life support. The family asked doctors to remove her from life support shortly thereafter.

As it turned out, Elizabeth had been fighting high cholesterol for 15 years, which led to her heart condition. *Her personal physician would have known this*—if he'd had the opportunity to see her on her previous visits. [24]

NICHOLAS KEANE

Still in a great deal of pain and weak from back surgery, 83-year-old Nicholas Keane was being discharged from the rehabilitation center his HMO had sent him to for recovery. According to his daughter, Sheila Christenen, Nicholas had trouble even getting out of bed, much less leaving the facility.

She knew her father needed more time to recover from the surgery, but she also knew she couldn't convince his HMO-backed doctor to allow him to stay.

Suspecting cost as the real issue, Mr. Keane's daughter found a "personal medical advocate" in California who represents patients in these types of cases. In the end, Mr. Keane's own treatment plan allowed him to stay at the rehabilitation center for 10–12 days, not the *five days* they initially dictated. In the end, Mr. Keane was able to recover fully and is now leading a healthy life.

As one doctor put it, "I get bonuses for keeping people away from specialists. I try not to read [the HMO guidelines]. They say: 'Don't use specialists. Don't refer out. Do as few lab tests as possible. Use cheaper drugs.' That's why I try not to read them." [25]

DR. ELLIOTT VICHINSKY

Dr. Elliott Vichinsky is an expert in sickle-cell anemia and runs a large program at the Children's Hospital in Oakland, California. He had a teen-age patient who not only had sickle-cell anemia, but also suffered from a complication that causes paralysis if not aggressively treated. The mother of the teen was on public assistance at the time. Dr. Vichinsky's treatments were working well for the teen, and the feared paralysis was held at bay with his procedures.

Then her mother got a job as a secretary, along with health benefits from an HMO. Her employer and the HMO told the mother that her daughter now had to be seen in a suburban hospital for her illness. A hematologist took over Vichinsky's work; however, he wasn't as experienced or skilled, and the mother immediately noticed a change in her teen's health.

The mother asked if her daughter could be returned to Dr. Vichinsky. The answer was no. Then Dr. Vichinsky himself called the HMO, explained the complications of the teen's disease, and asked to be allowed to continue his prior treatments. The answer was no.

The teen had a stroke and died under the care of the HMO's hematologist. [26]

BRENT RUFENER

Brent Rufener is the director of provider relations for Oregon Dental Services, a program that provides dental care to poor persons insured by the innovative Oregon Health Plan. In a memo sent out to his group of dentists caring for the poor, Rufener explained ODS's new policy:

"The dental office is confronted with OHP [Oregon Health Plan] patients who demonstrate neglect and desire immediate service. There must be strong emphasis on preventive care rather than immediate repair. As many of these individuals demonstrate significant neglect, repair must be postponed."

Rufener further explained that repairing the teeth of Oregon's most vulnerable citizens should be "postponed" for an inhumane *six months.*

In responding to Rufener, Ian Timm of the Oregon Primary Care Association notes that the policy "seems particularly uncaring and unprofessional. ODS is aware that 50 percent of the people covered by the Oregon Health Plan do not remain covered for more than six months. In a capitated environment, this policy reinforces the perception that managed care creates incentives to deny needed care." [27]

CHRISTY DEMEURERS

Like Nelene Fox, Christy DeMeurers was a member of HealthNet of Woodland Hills, California, and also had breast cancer. She also needed the expensive bone-marrow treatment, and it was covered in her policy.

Her request also was denied by her HMO, and she died—leaving behind a husband and two children who must console themselves with a $1.01-million settlement. [28]

SUSIE LOBB

"Susie Lobb became a widow at age 46. She blames her husband's death on his health maintenance organization.... In July 1993, Dwight Lobb was recovering from elective surgery ... in San Diego. 'I thought he was going to be well taken care of. I came home with complete peace of mind,' Susie Lobb says. 'Then I got a call at 1:30 a.m. from the surgeon. My husband was found dead.' It was his 47th birthday. The reason, says his widow: Hours after the surgery nobody noticed he was hemorrhaging internally. 'It was lack of the most basic care. No one checked him for over an hour and a half...He lost his life because no one came in his room and checked on him...[The HMO] settled with her for $400,000, attributing Lobb's death to 'judgment of individual nurses.' Lobb believes the HMO cut corners in caring for her husband." [29]

USA TODAY COVER STORY, OCT. 17, 1995

FROM THE HORSE'S MOUTH

"...Every time a capitated doctor performs a service or admits a patient to the hospital, it cuts into his income. If he spends less than the capitated rate, he pockets the difference; if he spends more, he eats the losses...." [30]

TIME, JAN. 22, 1996

"...HMOs already know the basic law of medical economics: The ultimate economy in medicine is death. So if they have a sick 70- or 80-year-old with a heart attack, a cancer and a stroke, an HMO will be tempted to think automatically of taking him out of his misery, say by 'forgetting' to prescribe an expensive heart medicine that can keep him alive." [31]

HARRY SCHWARTZ, MEDICAL WRITER/FORMER NEW YORK TIMES EDITORIAL BOARD MEMBER, QUOTED IN USA TODAY EDITORIAL, JULY 28, 1995

"...These organizations have jettisoned the old Marcus Welby-style medicine for something entirely new, in which doctors become 'gatekeepers,' patients become 'covered lives,' and remote managers decide who gets treatment and who doesn't..." (32)

TIME, JAN. 22, 1996

"...On Jan. 5 [an Oregon HMO] was slapped with $20,000 in state fines for improperly denying coverage of emergency room visits. State officials targeted [the HMO] because of its pattern of denying claims without proper investigation and then reversing a large portion of the cases upon appeal. [The HMO] is not the first and probably won't be the last HMO to be a target in the new battle over whether HMOs are too stingy. As insurers cinch the medical belt to squeeze what they consider inappropriate costs out of the system, consumers will feel the pain where sometimes it hurts the most—in the pocketbook. But that shift has raised concerns among consumers and state officials charged with protecting them." (33)

THE BUSINESS JOURNAL, JAN. 12, 1996

"...Prodded by large companies fed up with rising medical costs, the new medicine's entrepreneurs have turned health care into a corporate battlefield increasingly governed by the promise of stock market wealth, incentives that reward minimal care and a brand of aggressive competition alien to front-line doctors for whom dressing for success still means wearing khakis and a lab coat. No one disputes that managed care has at last put the brakes on medical spending, or that it has proved an effective vehicle for rationing health care, a profoundly sensitive subject in a culture raised on the notion that even the most expensive and esoteric treatments should be available to all....Yet the most fundamental question raised by the new medicine is one largely missing from public debate: Can you still trust your doctor?" (34)

TIME, JAN. 22, 1996

"...But savings may turn out to be illusory. Undertreating patients, sometimes with disastrous results, is inevitable. Medical decision-making is shifting from physicians to management. Patients will find it more difficult to trust their doctors, who may not be acting in their best interest." (35)

JOAN BECK, CHICAGO TRIBUNE SYNDICATE, JAN. 1996

"...It's a shift that has taken place a lot more quickly than patients are ready for—that's absolutely true. What's shifting is, patients can't drive it anymore; patients can't decide, 'My ear hurts, so I'm going to go to the doctor today.'" (36)

WILLIAM POPEK, CHIEF MEDICAL OFFICER, HEALTHNET
QUOTED IN *TIME*, JAN. 22, 1996

GAG CLAUSE

"Provider agrees to discuss all concerns, dissatisfactions, or disagreements with this agreement or the health plan directly with health plan, not the members. This section is not intended to restrict provider in discussing a member's medical condition, treatment with member, or financial agreement between physician and plan if requested by member. Provider agrees that violation of this provision shall constitute grounds for termination." [37]

At first glance, this little paragraph seems reasonable enough—but its purpose is much broader than a first reading may reveal. This is an example of a "gag clause," which can be found in many HMO doctor contracts; it's meant to keep patients in the dark about their care. This type of clause prohibits doctors, on threat of their job, from voluntarily discussing anything adverse about your health plan, including treatment options not covered by the plan— or even the need for a second opinion!

"The gag rule prohibits doctors from honestly telling the patient that they could give them different options—but the plan won't allow it," one lawyer notes.

Even an HMO executive has admitted it on the record: *"The gag rule is not in the patient's best interest."*

CHAPTER 8

STOP THE BLEEDING

You've now read about how traditional medical ethics have been perverted by HMO-insurance conglomerates, and how perverse financial incentives have corrupted the HMO physician's relationship with the patients. You've read about how you the patient are viewed as unimportant by your HMO, and how HMOs replace you, the primary driver of health care, with the almighty dollar.

The colossal scientific progress made by medicine in the past 50 years has been stunted by a new medical culture that doesn't allow the patient to enjoy the benefits of this progress. What good is it if we can save people's lives, when HMO managers don't allow gatekeepers to give their patients access to technology or specialists with the expertise? Because of the incredible penetration of aggressive managed care throughout the nation, many health-care professionals have thrown in the towel, believing it's too late to put a stop to the changes that have subverted medicine's morals.

But it's never too late to demand changes that protect you from unscrupulous medical practices that could result in injury and death. The system is clearly broken, but it's not irreparable. There are six steps we can take that will effectively draw a line in the sand for the patient:

1. ELIMINATE CAPITATION AND OTHER PERVERSE FINANCIAL INCENTIVES AIMED AT DENYING PATIENTS STANDARD MEDICAL CARE.

As you've clearly seen, capitation and the other financial incentives—given to doctors to bribe them away from helping their patients—will continue to harm patients throughout the country. Doctors cannot

**The doctor's conflict of interest can be resolved—
by eliminating capitation and other
perverse financial incentives.**

work for patients while at the same time working for
an HMO, an insurance company, the government, or
their own personal needs. *The doctor's conflict of
interest must be resolved, by not allowing perverse financial
incentives to play a role in health-care treatment decisions.*

The federal government has already recognized
the importance of this issue, and recently established
rules limiting the types of perverse financial incentives
given to doctors treating Medicare/Medicaid patients
in HMOs. These rules were established in order to
"protect patients against improper clinical decisions
made under the influence of strong financial

incentives" offered to doctors by HMOs. The rules also mandate that Medicare/Medicaid physicians buy insurance that limits the amount of money they can lose on any HMO patient, in order to curb doctors from maintaining a perverse financial incentive to skimp on care. [38]

Rules such as the ones implemented by the federal government are a good first step, but *all* perverse financial incentives that influence care decisions must be eliminated, both within public- and private-sector health care. A system by which a doctor is charged with keeping you well *and* declaring you well will always harm the patient.

2. FORCE INSURANCE COMPANIES TO SHARE LIABILITY WITH CONTRACTED PHYSICIANS WHEN CARE DECISIONS ARE BASED UPON PAYMENT.

Under most current HMO schemes, the insurance company—which is supposed to be responsible for paying your medical bills—gets away scot-free from any liability when they contract your care to an HMO or physician group. If your care becomes expensive, under an HMO the costs for paying for that care come out of the *physician's* pocket, giving that physician incentive to limit the amount of care you receive.

In the future, HMOs should share liability with physicians when twisted care decisions turn into "negative outcomes."

From stories such as Linda Peeno's (page 48) and others, it's clear that HMO insurance companies exert undue influence on clinical decision-making through their payment system. The physician is faced with an unholy choice: *Perform a costly procedure without payment and eventually go bankrupt, or buy into the HMO racket and begin withholding care.* In the latter scenario, only the physician is held liable if the patient has a "negative outcome" when not treated. Even though the treatment was denied due to the *insurance company's* unwillingness to pay for the procedure. Under these circumstances, the insurance company is also guilty—and should be held liable, along with the physician, for putting the patient at risk.

3. FAMILIES WITHOUT INSURANCE SHOULD PAY NO MORE PER PROCEDURE THAN FAMILIES WITH INSURANCE.

Here's a little-known fact: Many times, people with insurance pay significantly less per procedure than people without insurance—even when that procedure is performed by the same physician!

We're not talking about low premiums here—we're talking about the *real* cost of the procedure, before the insurance company's reimbursement is factored into the total. For example: A man needs cataract surgery, but doesn't have the insurance to cover it. So he starts shopping around and finds that the procedure will cost him $7,500 for each eye. However, the rate charged to insured patients is only $2,500 per eye! [39]

The reason non-insured patients pay more is to subsidize physicians who cut deals with insurance companies on their patients. The bulk of any physician's practice consists of insured patients. But the insurance company often cuts a deal with the physician to discount procedures and do work "at the margin," with no profit. In order to make up the difference,

**We need to stop letting doctors gouge
their uninsured patients to cover
the deficit caused by HMOs.**

some physicians overcharge their "uncovered" patients.

This is ethically wrong. Gouging uninsured people to supplement the books should be illegal. On principle, all patients should be treated equally—*regardless* of how they reimburse the doctor. And by removing this shady method of covering costs from physicians' lists of legal options, it will force them to confront the unreasonably low per-patient reimbursements provided by HMOs.

4. PROHIBIT TAX DISCRIMINATION BETWEEN FAMILIES AND CORPORATIONS.

Here's another little-known fact: Did you know that corporations get to buy health-care benefits for their employees with pre-tax dollars? In other words, these benefits are tax-free to corporate entities. However, individuals and families who buy their own insurance do so with *after*-tax dollars, costing them significantly more per policy.

Why, you ask? The answer dates back about 50 years, when the federal government implemented price and wage controls after World War II. As a concession to business, they gave them these tax breaks. Over the past 50 years, while salaries have increased along the same lines as inflation, benefits have skyrocketed, and have actually taken the place of pay increases. So there exists a discrepancy between corporate policies and private policies. This creates an unfair advantage that must be rectified and equalized if our health-care system is going to treat everyone equally.

A "medical savings account" (MSA) is one way
to put financial control of your medical destiny
back where it belongs—in *your* hands.

5. CREATE TAX-FREE "MEDICAL SAVINGS ACCOUNTS" (MSAs) THAT ALLOW HIGH DEDUCTIBLES AND CO-PAYMENTS.

What is a Medical Savings Account? An MSA is
exactly what it sounds like: a savings account established
just for paying your medical bills. Under the current
system of health-care insurance, you or your employer
pay a monthly premium to the insurance company. If
you don't go to the doctor, you never see that money
again; you lose that monthly fee. Under the MSA plan, if
you don't go to the doctor, *you keep the money in the
savings account; the money is yours!*

There are a number of different ways to set up a Medical Savings Account; however, a typical account might work like this:

Assume you pay $300 a month through your employer for health care for your family. Instead of giving all that money to the insurance company, you take that money and stick it into your personal Medical Savings Account. Within a year's time, you would have put $3,600 into that account to use for your family's health care needs. Under this scenario, you would use your Medical Savings Account to pay for doctor visits, prescriptions, laboratory tests, and other routine medical expenses incurred during that year.

Obviously, $3,600 is not going to be sufficient to cover major medical emergencies. So most people use a portion of their Medical Savings Account to purchase a catastrophic medical insurance plan that covers major medical emergencies. However, most families still will not spend $3,600 a year on medical costs. Under current insurance plans, you pay all that money and lose what you don't use. If your family is healthy and you don't need a doctor that year, you have lost the entire $3,600!

Medical Savings Accounts allow you, not the insurance company, to keep what you don't spend on health care. At the end of the year, the money left in your account can either be "rolled" over to the next year, or taken out for your family's other needs. Either way, you have saved money not spent on health care and you

Let's give the *patient* financial incentives to stay healthy—instead of giving the *doctor* financial incentives to ignore the sick.

haven't lost it to the insurance industry.

So with MSAs, if you need a special medical test you can get it without some HMO bean counter telling you no. The key to the MSA is that you and your family, not the insurance company, HMO, or government, decides what level of care you need and get. And with MSAs, what you don't spend you get to keep!

6. GIVE THE PATIENT, NOT THE DOCTOR, INCENTIVES FOR GOOD HEALTH.

As discussed in Chapter 6, the vast majority of

medical costs can be traced to lifestyle choices. If you smoke, drink, or eat fatty foods, you contribute to your own future ill health—which can cost quite a bit of money to repair, if it *can* be repaired.

Under the current system of medicine, there's no incentive for the patient to stay healthy beyond his or her own conscience. As an insured patient, you don't get *paid* for staying healthy, and if you get sick, you don't pay the majority of your medical bills— your insurer or HMO does. You're not really a player in your own health care; instead, the insurance company, HMO, and doctor all get a piece of your premium, regardless of your health.

A system must be devised in which the *patient*—not the other parties—receives incentives, savings, or other rewards for disciplined good health. For example, patients who don't smoke, drink, or have high cholesterol should receive lower health-care premiums. What patients don't spend of their health-care dollars should profit *them*, not their doctors!

If these six rules were adopted universally by the medical community, patients would once again control their health-care dollars, deciding for themselves which health-care service to buy.

These six steps, if implemented, also take into account the possibility of a national or global health-care crisis—something for which an HMO is woefully unprepared. History is rife with these sorts of plagues, from polio to smallpox to AIDS. *An HMO system only works when the majority of its clients are healthy.* A massive outbreak of any serious illness, under HMO policies, would bankrupt countless scores of physicians—unless, of course, those physicians denied care.

Under the proposed six rules, if there *was* health-care rationing to be done, the patient—not some bureaucrat with no stake in the patient's individual health—could choose what he or she could afford.

As you can see, together these six rules create a healthy medical system—at the same time adding protection, equity, and justice for patients and physicians, while keeping potential HMO abuses in check. If a family is uninsured, they should not be overcharged to cover paltry HMO reimbursements. And if a family can buy health care with the same taxation advantages as corporations—*and* be assured that their doctor isn't receiving financial incentives to deny the care they're trying to buy with their MSA— the system works to everyone's benefit.

IS BAD HEALTH CARE REALLY BETTER THAN NONE AT ALL?

There's an overwhelming belief in this country that bad health care is better than none at all. As a society, we seem content to allow our most vulnerable citizens to be placed in a health-care system that puts their very lives in danger during every encounter with their physicians. We favor rationing care to the poor. We have been programmed to chant the mantra of the HMO community: *"Traditional medicine bad; HMO medicine good."* We allow our own doctors to receive financial incentives to delay, withhold, and deny us

A national survey found that many Americans trust auto-repair shops and the federal government more than their HMOs.

the standard medical care we need. And we let the corporate giants of medicine and Wall Street take our money—giving us little or nothing in return.

But the vast majority of Americans also know that there's something *wrong* with our health-care system. That's why a national survey showed that many Americans trust auto-repair shops and the federal government more than they trust their HMOs! However, most people aren't able to put their finger on *why* they don't trust their HMO—simply because they're not privy to the details about how their HMO makes money.

But the federal government understands what's happening. That's why the Department of Health and Human Services recently established rules saying that HMOs are forbidden from offering financial incentives to doctors that in any way influence care decisions regarding Medicare patients.

The problem with this rule, however, is enforcing it. The Federal Bureau of Investigation (FBI) has begun looking at HMO fraud, but admits it's difficult to prosecute. The FBI explains that it's easy to see when a doctor is providing unnecessary procedures, but very difficult to document when a doctor withholds care from a patient—until it's too late. And HMOs have implemented shrewd policies to ensure that the patient knows as little as possible about his or her own health care. The result is that the patient doesn't even know whether care has been withheld or not. (40)

Even as the HMO community was pressuring Americans to buy into its brand of health care, one of their own broke rank last year, ripping a hole in the HMO community's dirty little secret. Physicians Health Services of Connecticut dropped the use of capitation and financial incentives in their HMO. "We get rid of some political minefields here, and we don't lose any money doing it," Chief Executive Officer Michael E. Herbert told the media. "We're doing it because the old way seemed to work just as well." (41)

HMOs don't really save significant money—they just take dollars meant for your health care and put them in the pockets of HMO executives.

Mr. Herbert is absolutely correct: *HMOs don't really save significant money!* A review of major research by the American Medical Association found "no evidence that managed care, in any form, has reduced the rate of growth in national health expenditures." In fact, the AMA further reported that if all medical care were delivered through HMOs, a safe estimate of savings would be *only 3.9 percent.* [42]

The HMO community has known this all along. Yet they continue to tell us they're saving tons of money in medical costs. The fact is, HMOs are having their cake and eating it too! Here's how they get away with it:

The money HMOs save in medical costs by not delivering care is *shifted* to HMO executives, stockholders, and Wall Street investors. *There's no true cost savings in HMOs, as the AMA clearly points out, because the money doesn't leave the system; the money simply is shifted to a different recipient.* It's like taking money out of your left pocket and putting it in your right!

There are two facts that prove this money is being shifted: First, managed health care executives are making *62 percent more* in pay and bonuses than heads of companies similar in size and performance. In other words, HMO executives are making a killing by shifting dollars meant for your care into their pockets. Second, managed-care stocks currently are one of the hottest commodities on the Stock Exchange. This means that publicly traded HMOs owe their allegiance to stockholders who demand profits, not patients demanding care. This slight-of-hand is nothing more than an accountant's cheap parlor trick, intended to make you believe that your HMO is saving you money—when in fact your HMO is reaping huge financial benefits in the hundreds of millions of dollars. [43]

Unfortunately, HMOs have found a number of willing accomplices to their scheme. The government, the insurance industry, your employer, your doctor, your hospital, and your pharmacist all benefit financially from the HMO model. This leaves you to fend for yourself in an increasingly dangerous health-care market. While the traditional medical model purposely created checks and balances between the doctor and insurance company in order to protect the patient, the HMO model purposely places the doctor and insurance company on the same side. This leaves no one to advocate for the patients—except the patients themselves.

Although going to the doctor has become a daunting proposition, there are a number of things you can do to help protect yourself from a system run amok. The following patient-protection formulas have been created by health-care professionals to help guide the unsuspecting patient through the gauntlet of HMO medicine.

QUESTIONS TO ASK BEFORE JOINING AN HMO

SOURCE: KAISER PERMANENTE [44]

CHOOSING A PERSONAL PHYSICIAN

- **Can I learn about the doctor's background and qualifications?**

TREATMENT DECISIONS

- **When I join the health plan, will I know what treatments are covered?**
- **Can my doctor tell me about alternative treatments?**
- **Can my doctor order a test, arrange a hospital stay, or refer me to a specialist without getting approval first?**
- **Is my doctor free from financial incentives that might limit care?**

COMPLAINTS

- **Does this health plan track complaints and respond to them quickly and appropriately?**
- **Is it easy to file a complaint?**
- **Does this health plan have a good track record on complaints filed with the state's insurance commissioner?**

PATIENTS'
BILL OF RIGHTS

SOURCE: ASSOCIATION OF AMERICAN PHYSICIANS AND SURGEONS [45]

1601 N. Tucson Blvd. Suite 9
Tucson, AZ 85716

All Patients should be guaranteed the following freedoms:

- To seek consultation with physician(s) of their choice;

- To contract with their physician(s) on mutually agreeable terms;

- To be treated confidentially, with access to their records limited to those involved in their care or designated by the patient;

- To use their own resources to purchase the care of their choice;

- To refuse medical treatment, even if it is recommended by their physician(s);

- To refuse third-party interference in their medical care, and to be confident that their actions in seeking or declining medical care will not result in third-party-imposed penalties for patients or physicians;

• To receive full disclosure of their insurance plan in plain language, including:

> CONTRACTS: A copy of the contract between the physician and health-care plan, and between the patient or employer and the plan;

> INCENTIVES: Whether participating physicians are offered financial incentives to reduce treatment or ration care;

> COST: The full cost of the plan, including co-payments, co-insurance, and deductibles;

> COVERAGE: Benefits covered and excluded, including availability and location of 24-hour emergency care;

> QUALIFICATIONS: A roster and qualifications of participating physicians;

> APPROVAL PROCEDURES: Authorization procedures for services, whether doctors need approval of a committee or any other individual, and who decides what is medically necessary;

> REFERRALS: Procedures for consulting a specialist, and who must authorize the referral;

> APPEALS: Grievance procedures for claim or treatment denials;

> GAG RULE: Whether physicians are subject to gag rules, preventing criticism of the plan.

PATIENT MANIFESTO

A broad coalition of patient and health-care-provider groups recently agreed on a set of standards by which managed-care organizations should treat their patients. Drafted by the National Health Council—which represents 103 groups, including the American Medical Association—this patient-rights agreement was opposed by the insurance industry, as well as by the major HMO trade organization. However, patients would be wise to heed the NHC's advice: [46]

PATIENTS HAVE THE RIGHT TO:

- Informed consent on treatment decisions, timely access to specialty care, and confidentiality protections;
- Concise, understandable information about coverage;
- An appeals process for coverage decisions;
- A reasonable choice of providers;
- Information about provider incentives or restrictions that might influence practice patterns.

PATIENTS HAVE THE RESPONSIBILITY TO:

- Pursue healthy lifestyles;
- Be knowledgeable about their health plan;
- Actively participate in treatment decisions;
- Cooperate fully with mutually agreed-upon treatments.

OREGON BALLOT INITIATIVE #35
1996 NOVEMBER GENERAL ELECTION
SPONSORED BY GORDON MILLER, M.D.

....

AN ACT

Be it enacted by the People of the State of Oregon:

PREAMBLE: Because patients have the right to be protected from unscrupulous practices which reward health care providers for withholding standard patient care, the following is enacted:

SECTION 1. A health care provider shall not be directly or indirectly compensated, except by an individual or family, for the delivery of health care according to any standard other than one or more of the following:

(A) Work performed
(B) An hourly wage
(C) Prearranged salary/benefits
(D) Bonuses based upon work performed
(E) Reimbursement for expenses

SECTION 2. After December 31, 1997, any health care provider who has not complied with Section 1 of this act shall have their business and professional license suspended until compliance is achieved.

SECTION 3. For the purposes of this Act, the following are defined:

(A) Health Care Provider

(1) Any individual or entity, including health care professionals and employers/contractors of health care professionals, directly or indirectly involved in the delivery of health care, but excluding insurers.

(2) A health care contractor, but excluding insurers.

(B) Work Performed

(1) The delivery of health care for specifically diagnosed/treated individual patient health care needs.

SECTION 4. These sections shall supersede any other provision of the Oregon Revised Statutes with which they conflict. If any subsection, clause or part of these sections is held invalid under the United States Constitution or Oregon Constitution as to any person or circumstance by any court of competent jurisdiction, the remaining subsections, clauses and parts shall not be affected and shall remain in full force and effect.

TOLL-FREE

MANAGED CARE (HMO)

COMPLAINT HOTLINE

1 (800) 800-5154

DO YOU HAVE AN HMO HORROR STORY?

...Where improper treatement or no treatment was given?
...Where tests were not performed when they should have been?
...Where non-medical personnel overrode the doctor's decision?
...Where care was put off and put off until it was too late?

If your answer is YES to any of these questions, or if you've encountered other problems, please call the *HMO COMPLAINT HOTLINE*. It's answered by a special voice-mail system, and the information you give will remain confidential. Your call will be returned, or you'll receive a written reply from a physician.

This hotline is sponsored by*Physicians Who Care*, a national organization of physicians who advocate for patients' rights.

GLOSSARY

Health Maintenance Organization (HMO): An organization of health-care providers, either contracted or salaried, who provide care to a population of patients delivered to the organization via group health insurance. Any managed care organization. *(NOTE: This definition has no relationship to federal rules and guidelines governing Health Maintenance Organizations.)*

Third-Party Payer: Any payer of health care other than the receiver of health care, i.e. the patient.

Insurer: Entity that takes a premium in order to pay for expenses of health care; entity that takes "risk" for patient's health.

Risk Pool: A pool of money collected from a group of doctors and third-party payers that is used to pay for tests, specialists, and hospital stays.

Medical Savings Account (MSA): A special tax-free savings account established in order to pay health-care costs.

"Medical Darwinism": A sarcastic term used to describe a medical system where the healthy thrive, and the sick are treated as second-class.

"Wall Street Medicine": Health care that is publicly traded on the stock market.

FOOTNOTES

1. *L.A. Street Stories* with Ed Bradley, 1995.

2. *Journal of the American Medical Association*, Volume 335, p. 21.

3. *The Oregonian*, Oct. 2, 1996.

4. *U.S. News and World Report*, Jan. 15, 1996.

5. *Time* Magazine, Jan. 22, 1996.

6. *Vandals at the Gates of Medicine* by Miguel A. Faria, Jr., M.D., Hacienda Publishing, 1994.

7. Anecdote from Gordon Miller, M.D.

8. Anecdote from Gordon Miller, M.D.

9. Anecdote from Gordon Miller, M.D.

10. *Vandals at the Gates of Medicine* by Miguel A. Faria, Jr., M.D., Hacienda Publishing 1994.

11. Father Ray Carey before the Archdiocese of Portland, OR, 1996.

12. *Northwest Reports*, KPTV, Portland, OR, May 5, 1996.

13. *Northwest Reports*, KPTV, Portland, OR, May 5, 1996.

14. *Vandals at the Gates of Medicine* by Miguel A. Faria, Jr., M.D., Hacienda Publishing, 1994.

15. *The Journal of the Medical Association of Georgia*, Miguel A. Faria, Jr., M.D., Vol. 84, April 1995.

16. Linda Peeno, M.D. Testimony before the United States House of Representatives House Committee on Commerce, May 30, 1996.

17. *Time* Magazine Jan. 22, 1996.

18. *The Oregonian*, Dec. 18, 1996.

19. *Dolin's Rules of Competition* by Leigh Dolin, M.D.

20. *L.A. Street Stories* with Ed Bradley, 1995.

21. *Newsweek*, Oct. 23, 1995.

22. *Newsweek*, Oct. 23, 1995.

23. *The Oregonian*, Dec. 5, 1995

24. *The Oregonian*, May 1, 1996.

25. *The Oregonian*, March 28, 1996.

26. Bob Herbert syndicated national column, July 15, 1996.

27. *Oregon Health Forum*, May 1996.

28. *Time* Magazine, Jan. 22, 1996.

29. *USA Today*, Oct. 17, 1995.

30. *Time* Magazine, Jan. 22, 1996.

31. *USA Today*, July 28, 1995.

32. *Time* Magazine, Jan. 22, 1996.

33. *The Oregon Business Journal*, Jan. 12, 1996.

34. *Time* Magazine, Jan. 22, 1996

35. Joan Beck, *Chicago Tribune*, January 1996.

36. *Time* Magazine, Jan. 22, 1996.

37. *Willamette Week*, March 12, 1996.

38. *AOA News*, April 22, 1996.

39. Anecdote from Gordon Miller, M.D.

40. *BNA Health Reporter*, Vol. 5, Number 25, Jan. 20, 1996.

41. Reuters News Service, May 22, 1996.

42. *American Medical Association News*, April 8, 1996.

43. *Statesman Journal*, Feb. 20, 1996.

44. *Associated Oregon Industries Business Viewpoints*, March/April 1996.

45. Association of American Physicians and Surgeons, Health Rescue Network Chicago Conference, July 1996.

46. *American Medical Association News*, Dec. 5, 1996.

ORDER FORM

SPEAK NOW OR FOREVER REST IN PEACE

Mail To: Gordon Miller

P.O. Box 925

Salem, OR 97308-0925

I would like to order _____ copies of *Speak Now or Forever Rest in Peace.*

_____ x $7.99 per copy = _____

NO. OF COPIES   + SHIPPING & HANDLING **$3.00**

TOTAL _____

Your Name: _____

Address: _____

City, State, Zip: _____

Day Phone: _____

PAYMENT METHOD

❏ Check

❏ Money Order

❏ Visa/MasterCard

Card No. _____

Expiration Date _____

Signature X _____

Please allow 2-4 weeks for delivery.

Or order online at http://www.amazon.com